Symbols of Canada

Flowers

Edited by Deborah Lambert

WEIGL PUBLISHERS INC.

Published by Weigl Educational Publishers Limited
6325 10 Street SE
Calgary, Alberta
T2H 2Z9

www.weigl.com
Copyright ©2010 WEIGL EDUCATIONAL PUBLISHERS LIMITED

Library and Archives Canada Cataloguing in Publication data available upon request.
Fax 403-233-7769 for the attention of the Publishing Records department.

ISBN 978-1-55388-925-0 (hard cover)
ISBN 978-1-55388-931-1 (soft cover)

Printed in the United States of America
1 2 3 4 5 6 7 8 9 0 13 12 11 10 09

Editor: Heather C. Hudak
Design: Kathryn Livingstone

All of the Internet URLs given in the book were valid at the time of publication. However, due to the dynamic nature
of the Internet, some addresses may have changed, or sites may have ceased to exist since publication. While the author
and publisher regret any inconvenience this may cause readers, no responsibility for any such changes can be accepted
by either the author or the publisher.

Every reasonable effort has been made to trace ownership and to obtain permission to reprint copyright material. The publishers
would be pleased to have any errors or omissions brought to their attention so that they may be corrected in subsequent printings.

Weigl acknowledges Getty Images as one of its primary image suppliers for this title.
Alamy: pages 16, 23 middle right; Provincial Government of New Brunswick: page 5 bottom.

We gratefully acknowledge the financial support of the Government of Canada through the Book Publishing Industry Development
Program (BPIDP) for our publishing activities.

Contents

Ontario

Northwest Territories

Saskatchewan

Prince Edward Island

Nunavut

Quebec

Yukon

What are Symbols?

A symbol is an item that stands for something else. Objects, artworks, or living things can all be symbols. Every Canadian province and territory has official symbols. These items represent the people, history, and culture of the provinces and territories. Symbols of the provinces and territories create feelings of pride and citizenship among the people who live there. Each of the 10 provinces and three territories has an official flower symbol. This is one of many symbols a province or territory can have.

Creating a Floral Symbol

In most cases, floral symbols refer to flowers. However, an entire plant may be used as a floral symbol. In Canada, floral symbols are chosen from among the **flora** of the country, province, or territory that they are meant to represent. Traditionally, the flora chosen as symbols are commonly found throughout the region they represent. However, flora that is not **indigenous** to the region may be chosen for historical reasons. Floral symbols can be recognized for historic, religious, or other reasons.

Floral symbols are sometimes included on other official symbols, such as coats of arms and flags.

Locating Provinces and Territories

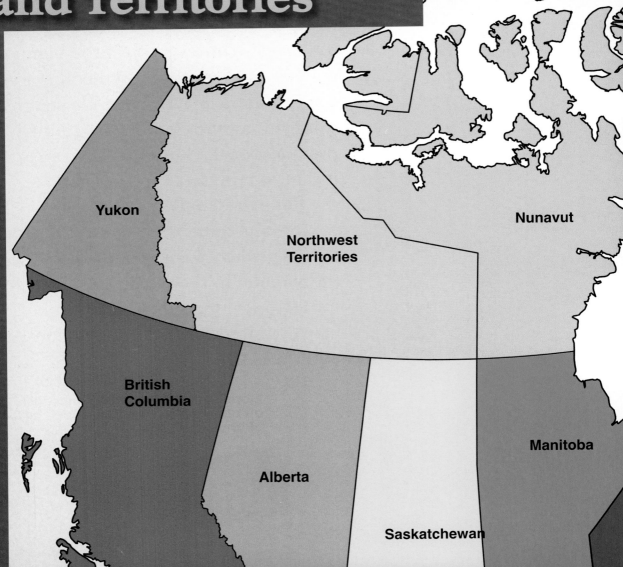

Each province and territory has a flower. Each province and territory is unique because of its land, people, and wildlife. Throughout this book, the provinces and regions are colour coded. To find a flower, first find the province or territory using the map on this page. Then, turn to the pages that have the same colour province or territory image in the top corner.

Web Crawler

Find out facts about each province and territory at **http://canada.gc.ca/othergov-autregouv/prov-eng.html**. Click on each province and territory.

Newfoundland and Labrador

Quebec

Ontario

Prince Edward Island

Nova Scotia

New Brunswick

Canada's Land and People

Canada is a large country. The ten Canadian provinces and three territories cover a vast amount of land. From one province or territory to another, the people, lifestyles, land, and animals are quite different. Each province and territory has its own identity. As a united country, Canada also has its own identity. Canada uses emblems to represent this identity.

Nova Scotia

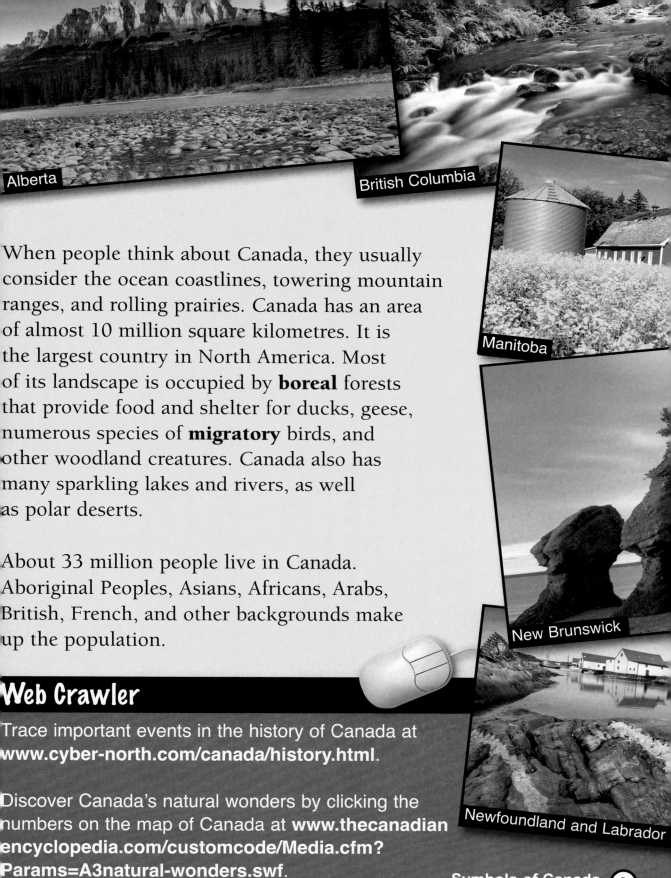

Alberta

British Columbia

Manitoba

When people think about Canada, they usually consider the ocean coastlines, towering mountain ranges, and rolling prairies. Canada has an area of almost 10 million square kilometres. It is the largest country in North America. Most of its landscape is occupied by **boreal** forests that provide food and shelter for ducks, geese, numerous species of **migratory** birds, and other woodland creatures. Canada also has many sparkling lakes and rivers, as well as polar deserts.

About 33 million people live in Canada. Aboriginal Peoples, Asians, Africans, Arabs, British, French, and other backgrounds make up the population.

New Brunswick

Web Crawler

Trace important events in the history of Canada at **www.cyber-north.com/canada/history.html**.

Discover Canada's natural wonders by clicking the numbers on the map of Canada at **www.thecanadian encyclopedia.com/customcode/Media.cfm? Params=A3natural-wonders.swf**.

Newfoundland and Labrador

Alberta

Alberta's floral symbol is the wild rose, or prickly rose. Schoolchildren chose the wild rose to be Alberta's provincial flower in 1930. That same year, it officially became the provincial flower by the Floral Emblem Act.

The wild rose grows throughout the province. It also grows across Canada, from Quebec to British Columbia. The wild rose is a pink flowering plant that grows up to 1.5 metres tall and has "bristle-like" branches. Its larger stems are thickly covered with small prickles. The wild rose blooms in late May and lasts until early August. Its petals are 3 to 5 centimetres in size and can be used to make perfume.

The wild rose is a useful flower. Many types of birds feed on its little red berries. Some people make tea and jam from wild rose berries. The tea is used as a medicine to fight colds and many types of infections. Aboriginal Peoples use the wild rose to heal skin infections.

British Columbia

The floral symbol of British Columbia is the pacific dogwood. It was adopted as the province's official flower in 1956. The pacific dogwood is the only Canadian floral symbol that is actually a tree. It is protected by law in British Columbia, and it is illegal to pick or destroy this tree there.

The pacific dogwood can be found in the province's southwestern forests. It is a small tree that grows 6 to 8 metres in height. Its leaves are dark green on the upper side and lighter on the underside. Thirty to forty small cream to greenish flowers appear in clusters and are surrounded by four to six large pointed, petal-like **bracts**.

The pacific dogwood blooms from April to May and, sometimes, again in the fall, when it produces bright red berries. These berries provide food for many birds and animals in British Columbia. The dogwood's strong wood is occasionally used for cabinetmaking and the handles of tools.

Manitoba

The floral symbol of Manitoba is the prairie crocus. Schoolchildren chose it as the province's official flower. On March 16, 1906, it became Manitoba's floral symbol. The flowers were named by early settlers who saw them growing in the prairie region.

Prairie crocuses begin to grow before the snow melts in the spring. They have pale blue or purple flowers rising from woody roots. These flowers are about 4 centimetres in diameter with five to seven petal-like **sepals**. When folded, the outer surface of the sepals appear to be covered in white, woolly hairs. The flowers remain open during the day but close at night. The leaves beneath are grey-green in colour. They only appear after the flowers fade.

Aboriginal Peoples used the prairie crocus to treat muscular pain. It was also used to stop nosebleeds and to treat infection in cuts and boils. The plant is dangerous if taken internally.

New Brunswick

New Brunswick's floral symbol is the purple violet. It is also known as the marsh blue violet. The purple violet was chosen as the provincial flower by the Women's Institute, the province's lieutenant governor, and schoolchildren. It was named New Brunswick's provincial flower in 1936. This flower can be found throughout New Brunswick, as well as other regions in Canada and the United States

The purple violet grows in moist meadows and along river banks. It blooms every year from May to July, and can grow to about 12.7 to 25.4 centimetres in height.

Jam and syrup are made from the purple violet's flowers. Some people use the flowers as medicine for colds and coughs.

Newfoundland and Labrador

The floral symbol of Newfoundland and Labrador is the **pitcher** plant. It is also known as the Indian dipper and the huntsman's cup. It was declared the official plant of Newfoundland and Labrador in 1954. Before becoming the official plant, it appeared on the Newfoundland penny in the 1880s.

The pitcher plant grows in bogs and marshes throughout Newfoundland and Labrador. It has one large, wine-red flower with a red and gold centre and hollow, pitcher-shaped leaves. These leaves are attached to the base of the stem. The flowers bloom in mid-summer and are about 3 to 7 centimetres wide. Pitcher plants eat insects, which become trapped inside the leaves when they fill with water.

Aboriginal Peoples used the pitcher plant to cure **smallpox** during colonial times. It also has been used for treating stomach ailments.

Northwest Territories

The white mountain avens is the floral symbol of the Northwest Territories. It was adopted as the official flower by the Council of the Northwest Territories when it enacted the Floral Emblem Ordinance in June 1957.

The mountain avens grows abundantly in the eastern and central Arctic, as well as in parts of the Mackenzie River region. It is found in open and well-drained areas, especially on high or rocky ground.

The mountain avens blooms in June and July. It is a small shrub that grows close to the ground. The mountain avens is a member of the rose family. Its narrow dark green leaves support a single white and yellow flower on a short stem. Each flower has eight to ten oval petals surrounding yellow **pollen grains**.

In the past, mountain avens were important to the Inuit. When the top of the mountain avens began to twist, the Inuit knew it was time to move inland to hunt caribou.

Nova Scotia

Nova Scotia was the first Canadian province to declare an official floral symbol. In 1901, the mayflower, also known as the trailing arbutus, was named Nova Scotia's floral symbol. This flower is only found in North America.

The mayflower derives its name from the Massachusetts pilgrims. It was the first flower of spring that they saw when they arrived in North America. They named it after the ship that brought them to Plymouth Rock. Every spring, its pink blossoms bloom on woody stems, hiding beneath heart-shaped evergreen leaves. These stems can grow from 15 to 30 centimetres long.

The mayflower is a symbol of Nova Scotia's success. Throughout the 1800s, it was celebrated in both song and poetry and was used to decorate the stamps and coins of Nova Scotia.

Nunavut

The purple saxifrage is the floral symbol of Nunavut. It was named the territory's official flower on May 1, 2000. It is beneath the caribou on Nunavut's coat of arms.

The purple saxifrage grows low to the ground, in gravel and cracks in rocks. It blooms from April to July and is usually the first flower to show its purple blossoms in the Arctic spring. These purple blossoms consist of five **spatula**-shaped petals that are about 5 to 15 millimetres in length. The flowers live for only 12 days.

The purple saxifrage has small, leathery oval-shaped leaves, which are about 3 millimetres long. These leaves have tiny, stiff hairs along their edges and appear as four overlapping rows on a stem.

When purple saxifrage are in full bloom, the Inuit know that young caribou are being born on the land. They use the flowers to make dye and the stems and leaves to make tea. The flowers are eaten, especially in communities where berries are not abundant.

Ontario

Ontario's floral symbol is the white trillium. In 1937, it was officially adopted as the province's floral symbol. The white trillium is found in the **deciduous** forests and woodlands of Ontario. The image of a trillium is found on the official logo of the provincial government and on the Franco-Ontarion flag. Its white blossom is associated with peace and hope.

Trilliums are also called wake robins. They bloom in late April and May when robins begin to return to Ontario after the winter. The white trillium grows to a height of 20 to 40 centimetres. Three white petals form the flower, with three green sepals underneath. The leaves are egg-shaped and also occur in groups of three. The white flowers are very sensitive to light and usually bend toward the Sun as it moves across the sky. As the flowers age, they turn pink.

Trilliums were used by Aboriginal Peoples for food and as medicine to help the sick. The leaves can be cooked and eaten, similar to spinach.

Prince Edward Island

The floral symbol of Prince Edward Island is the stemless lady's slipper. It was officially adopted as the province's floral symbol on April 25, 1947. On the coat of arms, lady's slippers surround the star. They represent early European settlers.

The lady's slipper is a type of orchid. It gets its name from the shape of its petals, which form a pouch that looks like a slipper.

The lady's slipper blooms in Prince Edward Island's wooded areas in late May and June. It mostly grows in shady and moist woodlands. The flower of the stemless lady's slipper is usually pink, although a white variety also occurs. Its leaves are thick, hairy, and appear **plaited**. It is illegal to pick lady's slippers on Prince Edward Island because they are becoming rare flowers.

Quebec

The blue flag iris is the floral symbol of Quebec. It replaced the Madonna lily as Quebec's provincial flower in November 1999. The blue flag iris was chosen as the provincial flower because it looks similar to the French **fleur-de-lis** symbol. This indigenous spring flower grows on more than half of Quebec's territory, from the St. Lawrence Valley to the shores of James Bay.

The blue flag iris blooms from May to June, and can be found growing along the edges of waterways and in moist soil. The purplish blue flowers are large. Each stem has sword-shaped leaves about 1.3 to 2.5 centimetres in width and bears two or more flowers. The blue flag can grow up to 1 metre tall. Its thick, fleshy **rootstock** produces many long, fibrous roots.

When not in bloom, blue flag resembles the plant sweet flag. Sweet flag is sometimes used in medicines and as a fragrance. Blue flag, however, is thought to be poisonous.

Saskatchewan

Saskatchewan's floral symbol is the western red lily, or prairie lily. It became the province's floral symbol in 1941. Its fiery red petals stand out against the green meadows, roadside ditches, and edges of bluffs where it grows.

The western red lily blooms from late June to mid July. A single flower or small cluster of flowers forms on the top of tall stems, which can grow to heights of 20 to 60 centimetres. The flowers are bright orange to almost red and are dotted with black near the base of the petals. The leaves are usually long and straight along the stem, with a **whorl** along the stem base. The western red lily is a rare flower that is protected by law.

The Plains Cree peoples and early settlers used the western red lily for food and medicine. The steamed roots were sometimes eaten instead of potatoes. Tea made from the plant was used to treat coughs, fevers, and stomach disorders.

Yukon

Fireweed, also known as blooming sally, was named the Yukon's floral symbol on March 27, 1957. It is called fireweed because it is the first flower to grow after a forest fire. This purple flower grows all over the Yukon, along the sides of roads, in forest clearings, and on land that has been burned by fire.

Fireweed blooms from mid-July to September. Each flower has four magenta, or dark reddish-purple, petals. Many flowers grow on the top of a single, tall stem, which can reach 50 to 200 centimetres in height. The large purple, magenta, or occasionally white flowers blossom from the bottom up. The fireweed has long, narrow, willow-like leaves.

All parts of fireweed can be eaten. People cook and eat sprouts of fireweed as greens. Bees produce a delicious honey from the flowers of fireweed.

Guide to Canada's Flowers

THE NATIONAL FLORAL SYMBOL
No offical symbol

ALBERTA
wild rose

BRITISH COLUMBIA
pacific dogwood

MANITOBA
praire crocus

NEW BRUNSWICK
purple violet

NEWFOUNDLAND AND LABRADOR
pitcher plant

NORTHWEST TERRITORIES
mountain avens

NOVA SCOTIA
mayflower

NUNAVUT
purple saxifrage

ONTARIO
white trillium

PRINCE EDWARD ISLAND
lady's slipper

QUEBEC
blue flag iris

SASKATCHEWAN
western red lily

YUKON
fireweed

Canada's National Floral Symbol

National emblems are symbols that are used for the entire country. The Canadian flag is one such symbol. Another is the common loon, which is the the national bird. The maple is the national tree. Canada does not have a national floral symbol, but the maple leaf is one of Canada's national symbols.

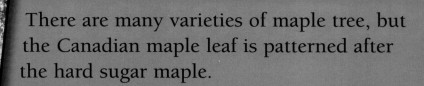

There are many varieties of maple tree, but the Canadian maple leaf is patterned after the hard sugar maple.

With the proclamation of Canada's new flag in 1965, the maple leaf has become Canada's most prominent symbol.

During both World War I and World War II, Canadian troops wore the maple leaf on their badges. It appears carved on the gravestones of fallen soldiers.

History of the Maple Leaf

As early as 1700, the maple leaf was used as a Canadian symbol. It was proposed as a symbol of Canada in 1834, when the Société Saint-Jean-Baptiste was founded. It was adopted again as a national symbol for the visit of the Prince of Wales in 1860. The maple leaf's national symbolism was widely understood by the time Alexander Muir wrote *The Maple Leaf Forever* in 1867. The maple tree was officially recognized as a national symbol in 1996.

Parts of a Flower

A flower is part of a plant. Most of Earth's plants have flowers that make seeds so that new plants can grow. Flowers come in many different sizes, shapes, and colours. Still, they all share the same basic traits.

PETALS Petals are the main parts of a flower. They come in many shapes and are often brightly coloured. Petals contain oils that give a flower its scent. This helps attract birds and insects to the flower. By brushing against the flower's centre, these animals help move pollen from the stamens to the pistil, which makes seeds.

STEM The stem holds the flower up. It also moves water, food, and minerals through the plant.

SEPAL Sepals are small, leaf-like parts below the petals. Sepals protect the flower as it grows. Most sepals are green. Others are colourful and are sometimes mistaken for petals. The western red lily, for example, is a flower with very colourful sepals. Some flowers, such as tulips, have no sepals at all.

STAMEN Stamens are the male parts of a flower. They grow in a ring around the pistil. Stamens make pollen. A seed grows when pollen from a different flower contacts the pistil.

PISTIL The pistil is the female part of a flower. It grows at the very centre of the flower. The pistil makes seeds with help from the stamens.

Test Your Knowledge

1 What is a floral symbol?

2 What is the floral symbol of Alberta?

3 Which province's floral symbol is a tree?

4 Which floral symbol remains open duing the day, but closes at night?

5 What is another name for the floral symbol called the Indian dipper?

6 In which province is the purple violet the floral symbol?

7 Which floral symbol survives by eating insects?

8 When does the mountain avens bloom?

9

Which floral symbol derived its name from the Massachusetts pilgrims?

13

From which flower do bees produce honey?

10

Which floral symbol is thought to be poisonous?

14

Which floral symbol's roots are sometimes eaten instead of potatoes?

11

In which province is the blue flag iris the floral symbol?

15

Which floral symbol blooms when robins return to Ontario?

12

Which floral symbol is a type of orchid?

Answers:
1. A flower or entire plant representing a country, province, territory, nation, or state
2. Wild, or prickly, rose
3. British Columbia
4. Prairie crocus
5. Pitcher plant
6. New Brunswick
7. Pitcher plant
8. June and July
9. The mayflower
10. Blue flag iris
11. Quebec
12. Lady's slipper
13. Fireweed
14. Western red lily
15. White trillium

Create Your Own Floral Symbol

Create a flower symbol to represent your community or school. Begin by thinking about what type of flower you want. Use this book to help you. What kinds of flowers grow in the region where you live? Will your flower grow in the ground, on a shrub, or on a tree?

Think about how your flower will look. Will your flower be large or small? How many petals will each blossom have? What colours will your flower be? Why? Look at the pictures in this book for help. You can also view thousands of plant and flower images online at **www.wildflower.org/bibliography/ show.php?id=928**.

Draw your flower on a piece of paper. Use the diagram on pages 26 and 27 to help you design the parts of your flower. Colour your drawing with felt markers or crayons. When you are finished, label the parts of your flower.

Write a description of your flower. What kind of flower is it? Where does it grow? What does it say about you?

Further Research

Many books and websites provide information about provincial and territorial floral symbols. To learn more about these symbols, borrow books from the library, or surf the Internet.

Books

Most libraries have computers that connect to a database for researching information. If you input a key word, you will be provided with a list of books in the library that contain information on that topic. Nonfiction books are arranged numerically, using their call number. Fiction books are organized alphabetically by the author's last name.

Websites

Find fun facts about each of Canada's provinces and territories at **www.pco-bcp.gc.ca/aia/index.asp?lang=eng&page= provterr&sub=map-carte&doc=map-carte-eng.htm**.

Learn about Canada's other emblems and symbols at **www.patrimoinecanadien.gc.ca/pgm/ceem-cced/symbl/ index-eng.cfm**.

Learn more about flowers, their uses, and meanings at **www.familymanagement.com/holidays/flowers/index.html**.

Make fun flower crafts using the instructions at **www.enchantedlearning.com/crafts/flowers**.

Glossary

boreal: northern regions with very cold temperatures

bracts: leaves, usually small, growing just below a flower

deciduous: trees that shed their leaves each year

fleur-de-lis: a lily illustration that has three petals that are tied together at the base; a symbol of France

flora: all the plant life of a given place or time

indigenous: from a certain place naturally

migratory: to move from one place to another

pitcher: a large container with a handle and a lip for pouring liquids

plaited: made by braiding or intertwining into a pattern

pollen grains: structures produced by plants containing male reproductive cells

rootstock: the root or part of the root used to produce plants

sepals: usually green parts that surround and protect the bud and extend from the base of a flower after it has opened

smallpox: a disease that causes sores on the skin

spatula: a kind of tool with a broad, flat, flexible blade

whorl: a circular arrangement of leaves or flowers around the stem of a plant

Index